Pranic Poetry:

Annals of one soul's journey,
closer towards the light...

Scott Hastie

Pranic Poetry by Scott Hastie
First published 2020
Centuria, London

ISBN: 9780992709334
e book ISBN: 9780992709341

A catalogue record for this book
is available from the British Library.

instagram scottie131313
twitter @scotthastiepoet
facebook.com/scotthastiespiritpoet

www.scotthastie.com

To kiss the fruit
And caress the flower,
To taste without tarnishing
Humble nature's natural dower,
In this sweet pursuit
I shall place my frail body
Till death's timely hour,
And do so
With only breath remaining
To wish that,
Amidst the winds of the world,
It will not shake nor cower
In the face of quiet eternity.

If you listen

If you listen carefully
There's a constant purr
In your soul,
With ambitions
Of provoking a response,
Akin to a mother
Forever nudging
Her fledglings forward
Into the light.

And this is reassuring,
As it's meant to be,
Putting the lie
To insignificance
Being the essence
Of our existence,
When the truth
Is quite to the contrary.

All this a gift
Easy to accept,
When such benevolence
Holds so steady,
Just waiting to be noticed,
Like the soft sigh
Of a tender young tree
In the gentlest
Of summer breezes.

If you are

If you are in a place
Where nothing seems right
And every moment hurts,
The sky is without colour,
Without hope,
Then paint it another way!

This time more honestly,
More bravely.

Paint the pictures
You need to find peace,
Knowing it is the truth
That has brought you here
To this point.

And yes, accepting
That truth is hard.

But this is the way,
Inch by exquisite inch,
The humble and generous
Amongst us live.

And one day
Get to discover
That the extraordinary
Is indeed possible.

In a world

In a world
That is far from certain,
This is for all lovers
Still to set forth,
Or imagining
They've yet to arrive.

This fitful journey
Of ours
No sideshow,
Albeit part
Of an ingenious conceit
That draws us tenderly
Towards the light,
Where chances
Can be so sweet
And every joyous release
Cannot help
But seed another.

So here it is!

And there
It ever was too,
Oh, but we knew it then.

Such sublime mapping,
The code of tomorrow
Already built into
All our yesterdays.

To live

To live a little
You have to die a little,
So says the angel's
Enigmatic smile.

Never was the need
For any anvil of angst
Upon which
To crack open
The coded chronicles
Of such a pointed
Lifetime dilemma.

Till then, limited
By such dominant
Conviction
That fears the end so.

And such
Are all our hopes,
Freer to flower
Brighter still
When no longer
Clad thus.

Every true passion
Shared since
Speaking so clearly
To this,
The resolute
Onward journey
Of our soul.

Passing

Passing,
So often fruitlessly,
Through all the doors
To desire in life,
Far finer,
Faraway prizes
Twist and tease still,
Like runaway kites
Caught up
In a storm of being
That only
More stillness
Can becalm.

Oh, for an end
To such struggles!

And with kind
Devotion
Comes just that.
An embrace
Of perfect peace
That never fails
To usher in
Its own mysteriously
Unforeseen reward.

Blanket upon blanket
Of selflessness,
Nestled now securely
In the glowing casket
Of your soul.

Where, deep therein
Forever,
Lies the warmest
And truest of dividends.

The lingering presence
Of love
Beneath the fragile,
Needy contours of us all.

An old view

An old view
Seen anew.

Lost
In morning perfection,
The illusion
Peacefulness
Improves everything,

When fervour's
A resource
Used all too sparingly
And there's
So much wonder
Out there
To even ruffle
The surface of.

How often
Do we turn away
Though?
Timid, as we are.

And without such sparks
Time can pass by,
Like an empty whisper,
Meaningless and negligent.

Till, all at once,
There you have it,
Pulsing within you,
The day of days!

Whatever else
Might come your way,
This you will always know.

Never rewarded thus
Unless you sing so.

A sheen

A sheen, a glow,
A charisma of sorts.

All we've come to know,
To touch the essence of,
Leaving behind a memory,
A presence of its own.

Energies
That eventually settle.

Coming to rest somehow
In the very fabric
Of who we are.

I see this so clearly
In the eyes of others.

Every moment
That has gone before
Bringing us here,
My friend.

And yet with so much
Still left to absorb.

Joy and pain
Spread so evenly
Along time's heavy arch.

Somewhere

Somewhere
There's never a sigh,
The choicest of gifts
Are always given,
Never chosen.

Our precious being
So much more
Than a vessel to fill,
When the world
Is so awash
With opportunity.

So dare to ignite
Fires of joy
Wherever you are,
Even if all
You might then
Be tempted to wish
Could well
Be yours forever,
Will one day
Be lost to you
In a changing of the light.

One in, one out,
It's a rum do!

Along with the fear
Of being forsaken
Or forgotten.

This will never happen
To a generous heart.

We are all prophets

We are all prophets
Of our own existence
Are we not?

And come what may,
Tis always
Such noble ambition
To leave telling traces
Of ourselves
Wherever we can.

Thus do all our lives
Become
An enduring tapestry
Of pointed moments,
Albeit seeded with loss,
The ache of which
Will pass,
Whilst such sweet emotion
Remains.

See how potently
That narrative runs on!

And to guide us on our way,
Amidst the endless sway
Of needs and desire,
Delicate patterns made,
Filigrees of real meaning.

The absolute truth
Of raw emotions
Etched on our heart,
Left behind,
Radiant,
As pathways to tomorrow.

Like the curiously

Like the curiously
Regal stance
Of a proud young deer,
Surveying
The early morning mists,
At any given moment
I am an aggregate,
The absolute sum of all
That has gone before.

And even
When I'm no more,
I will remain still
In every facet of place,
Of presence, of purpose,
Of breath
And bare beings too,
Any of which
And each of whom,
Would never have been
Quite as they are
Destined to be now
Had I not come
To settle here
Awhile too.

So well before the time
To slip away
Gathers much pace,
So should we all
Endeavour to love,
To leave
The best of ourselves behind.

And forever remember
The need to be kind.

Or else, who knows
What quiet despair
Might otherwise live on
In the still beating hearts
Of others.

What is this life

What is this life?
If it is not
As if to walk
Weightless
In this thin, bright air.

Openly and lightly
Like children
You know...

Simple joys,
Easily found,
That resonate
Beyond all measure.

Thus are we ushered
Gently into this world
And then challenged
To find our way home again
With our hearts open,
To where heaven knows
There are pearls awaiting.

Along with the chance,
Day by gleaming day,
To come to realise
The more generously
We shine,
The more we will
Blossom and prosper
Along a path
Where how stunning
It is to still be alive
When, just once in a while,
Those who could never sing
Suddenly can!

And as you pause
To marvel at that,
Best to know all those
Who similarly bless you
In faith
Helped make it so.

See how boundless love
Brings time to its knees.
A gift beyond compare.

Sweet meadows

Sweet meadows
Inspire broad smiles
On the face
Of the mountains beyond.

And sometimes it seems
Your blissful heart
Might stop
As, in the silence of time
And the generous
Whisperings
Of each passing year,
People come and go
In a celestial glow.

So by all means
Love who you love
The most readily,
Sit and drink
And laugh together,
Be a living embodiment
Of life's sweet dream.

But then, truly come
To be yourself
In a moment of grace,
Born of kindness.

For to step aside
And offer
The hand of rescue
To others
Is a gift beyond rubies.

Especially for those,
The sad and suffering
Amongst us,
Who so clearly
Have been
Other than this.

Glowing,
Earlier in their journey.

And can be again.

Pray

Pray,
Let all negative shapes,
Patterns,
Thought forms
Dissolve, disintegrate,
Be gone.

For, in the imagining,
We are the source
From which springs
All that ensues.

So don't ever pass by
The chance to lie back
In the long fragrant
Summer grass,
Gaze up
At the clear blue sky
And take the time
To feel what truly sings.

And yes, my friend,
Discover
It's all still there too,
Resonating,
So fluidly within you!

For, meander
As we might,
Scarred and feeble
As we all are,
We are never broken.

Always able
To be as one,
Whenever
We can gather
The courage
And summon up
The open heart to be so.

Sometime bruised

Sometime bruised
By the very air I breathe,
In the ceaseless
Crush of life,
When all that has been,
And will be no more,
Dallies still.

And truly
Moving forward
Can seem
Like a never ending
Series of encounters
With the intangible,
Too often
Just out of reach.

There comes a prayer
In my heart
As if to usher me
Affectionately
Towards a finer state
Of being,
Far beyond all notions
Of self doubt.

And then, Yes!
I see that you are here.

As if to hold my hand,
Cushion a tear,
Nurture my hopes,
Allay my fear.

How wonderful that,
Come what may,
Your timeless presence
Hovers so loyally
Over me still,
Like the loss
Of a sweet romance
Just waiting,
Oh so patiently,
To be rekindled.

Your beguiling smiles
And knowing laughter too!
The sweetest and most loving
Of reminders
That, for all the joy
And sorrows
I've bled and yearned for,
Soaked in equal measure,
How blessed am I
These days to be thus.

When so many
Poor souls
Amongst us
Lead such lives
Of quiet desperation
And die with their song
Still unsung inside them.

Stranded

Stranded,
As we are here
In defined space
No more than on lease to us
To enjoy such fine
And temporary congress in,
See how we have
The temerity to imagine
We are the finished being,
One and all!

Whereas,
If we only knew,
We are the initiate.
And on borrowed time too!

A precious seed
Of opportunity implanted.

Suspended somewhere
Between life
As we find it
And the soaring dance
Of the soul.

And as for energies
Already spent,
What do they
Count for now,
If not this very moment?

A far brighter flame
Still flickers within.

Take deep refuge

Take deep refuge
In a noble silence
That's best used to
Affirm the miracle
Of being alive,
When the simple act
Of pausing
To breathe in
The early morning air
Can only help you shine.
Bringing with it,
As it does,
The power to nourish,
To heal and transform.

All this
Not hard labour,
My friend,
When you can be
Joyous anywhere,
Free from any anxiety
About the future
Or regrets from the past.

For with your heart
And soul open,
Here and now,
In the stillness before you,
Can be found
The very wonder of life itself.

To catch sight

To catch sight
Of something telling
And quite often
Paradoxical,
Out of the corner
Of your eye.

Something
You feel so sure
You recognise,
You sense you might
Have seen before,
But haven't.

Something that's
More often than not
Elliptically mysterious,
Just as a luminescent lake
Would be
At the bottom of some dark
And turbulent ocean,
Only recently fathomed.

Such is
The language of light.

And, consciously
Prompted or not,
It works like this.
Plumbing our souls.

Inspiration,
In this way,
Endlessly
Only one shining
Moment away.

And seeded deep...

Thus do we
Discover ourselves.

Our true passion.

What a shame

What a shame
Never yet
To scale that wall,
When in truth
We are the only ones
Guarding it.

Though the will
To do so
Clings on still
In the very depths
Of our being,
Hard wired to our souls,
Like fluttering pennants
On a bloodied battlefield.

Talismans till then.
And that first
Bitter taste of defeat,
We never knew we had.

Here to remind us,
Even if only
Ever guaranteed
What so often seems like
The one oft
Despairing life,
Heaven can still be
Here and now.

And in just such
A valiant awakening
Can we revive
Ourselves,
Striding on towards
Such a precious land!

Wherein to learn
Everything,
But everything,
Is a given in our own hand.

We are stronger than we know.

See how

See how,
Around
The stream's
Silvery edge,
Reflected light
Dances on the surface
Of rushing water.

Becoming
The very essence
Of life
And motion itself,
Effortlessly tapping
Into timeless truths
That, once absorbed,
Echo right back
At you
More than ever before.

And with a peerless
Reminder
That's both soothing
And humbling
Of how,
In a single lifetime,
One could never oneself
Accumulate
Such knowing grace,
Gather up such melody,
Nor offer such endless
Nourishment.

Still here
With the chance
Of some
Sweet release though.

And, for so many
Amongst us,
Would that it were so!

To dream
That one day
Within
Such a river might flow.

As you raise

As you raise your gaze
To the heavens
And what light there is
Streams on through,
You only need
A moment's clarity
To grasp this
For what it is.

All at once,
The stars
Seeming to fall gently
From the skies
Melting
Into the soft, wet grass
At your feet.

Therein lies
The essence of existence
Complete before you.

And in all
Its constituent parts too.

This then
What it means
To offer up
A ringing prayer
Of hope,
My friend.

To ever have
The chance
Of being part of
That siren song again.

The rarest of entities,
As we all are,
On a permanent quest
Back to where it all began.

Woe

Woe is the person
Whose heart
Has not learnt,
Whatever the cost,
To love.

For even
The most damaged spirit
Can always be mended.

Renewed
By every act of compassion
Till the final breath fails
And eternity feels,
Albeit only for a moment,
Heavy upon your shoulders.

So, whatever
The likelihood
One might bleed,
Indeed
Collect some scars
Along the way!
Embrace this risk
Whilst you still can.

Certain as you can be
That our deepest wounds
Are often
Where the light best gets in.

Otherwise, what to do?

When, without
That leap of faith,
Every chance
Can so easily
Run away from us,
Like guttered water
Down some dingy drain.

Leaving behind
No vivid stain
Of proud purpose,
No lasting mark of living
Upon the world.

The well of being

The well of being
And, come what may,
The fathomless
Grace therein,
Reminds us
For every
Sombre moment
That can sometime
Envelop us,
There will soon be
Another on its way
To prick us with joy.

So however hollow
You might
Sometimes feel,
Please don't be tempted
To overlook
That stunning certainty.

Nor indeed
Ever think
To turn the lost,
The sad,
Nor the needy away
From your door,
For they could well be
Angels in disguise.

Faithfully follow instead
The ever generous
Whisperings of your soul,
Till your heart gathers
Fresh lustre
And sings again.

Here we are

Here we are then,
Like it or not.
Inescapably
Part of this world,
Every last element...

And with little option then
But to accept suffering
Sometimes
Has to be our lot,
When this
Fevered domain of ours
Is so often full
Of sound and fury,
Signifying nothing.

Beyond this though,
Through all the dense
Jungles of doubt,
And sometime despair,
There has to be the will
To shift inside,
A way forward to faith
Of some kind.

As if, this minute,
We should joyously
Embrace all we are
Together,
Our talismans too;
The very ground
We stand upon,
And fashion from this
Something shiny anew,
Of infinitely more value,
Or so we might hope...

But in the midst
Of such struggles,
I am often touched
And weep fond
Smiles of recognition,
Just remembering your face
On that first blessed day,
Recalling the importance
Of love given.
And that sense of pattern
Repeating itself,
Again and again,
Till, for the time being
At least,
All our energies
Are spent
And our lives no more.

The practice

The practice of
True religion
A very simple one.

It's essence
Being the story
Of how you live through
Each moment
Of every single day.

And, in this sense,
Like it or not,
We are all
Lamp holders
Caught
Within its thrall,
The ceaseless flicker
Of the soul.

And whatever
Comes of this,
My friend,
What all-pervading
Good fortune it is
To be so charged.

Even if, embedded
Within the very core
Of such blessings,
Is the insistence
That the best
Of who we are
Must cohabit
So closely
With the worst
Of ourselves,
To fully meet
This challenge.

And therein
Lurks a shadow.

Which, in itself,
Explains why
Any savoured acts
Of generosity,
Of pure,
Unfettered goodness
And compassion,
Never fail to have impact,
To draw real power
From the very ether itself.

A striking reminder
Of just how valuable
And powerful
Each and everyone one
Of us can be,
But that we knew
And truly understood it
To be so.

Our heads
And hearts too
Having long since
Lost all sense and sight
Of the delight in death
And the joyful release
It surely brings.

Devoted or not my friend,
One day this
We will all come to know.

Almost unnoticed

Almost unnoticed,
Honey on my lips.

Everyday anew
In the clean,
Sharp air,
The fresh dew of morning.

A profusion
Of life's finer nuances
Only just
Beginning again
To slip
Their welcoming fingers
Gently through my soul.

Highlighting times
When all thoughts
Of past,
Present and future
Begin to overlap
And any shadows made
Simply fall to the ground,
Only to dissolve
Into dancing leaves,
Soon lost
On a joyous breeze.

Tis the same
For everyone of us,
My friend,
Seeker or not.

And whatever
Iron-clad hesitation
May well still
Be loitering
Heavily in your heart,
One day
We will all achieve
Release.

Making this,
The final leg
Of our journey,
To where much lighter,
And far softer,
Sumptuous answers
Lie within.

Till then,
With each moment
Of elevation
Such as this,
Tantalisingly close.

Look deep

Look deep
Into your own self,
As life,
Its challenges,
Its gentleness too,
Runs its course
Kindly
Through your
Many chequered spirit.

And therein
Catch sight
Of something
Seemingly infinite,
A kaleidoscope
Of blossoming feelings
And emotion.

Recalling
After the event,
As we are always
Mysteriously
Able to do,
Just how
Such sudden despair,
Or indeed delight,
Can sometime
Creep upon us
Like twilight.

Often arriving
With such delicacy
We might not,
At first, even notice.

Conscious,
As we are,
That if we weren't,
From time to time,
So troubled,
So tested, so fallen,
We wouldn't be
Mortal at all!

Forever hankering
After sweet relief.
Such is devotion,
Love, compassion.

And realising this,
See how we come
Much closer than ever
From being just
One step away
From Earth's great gains.

A first glimpse of
The infinite garden within.

Quite from

Quite from where
You come from,
I know not,
But you have
Always been
A saviour to me.

Usually arriving
In the form of
What seems
So often
To be a child's voice
Whispering,
Sharp in the gloom.

A telling rejoinder
To whatever darkness
Still lurks within,
That all such burdens
Must, one day,
Fall away.

Like a spent sheath,
A shabby coat,
An old garment of sorts,
Not needed anymore.

Ultimately,
Everything
Will turn to gold
If it's allowed to.

In a migration home
To light and love
That's forever waiting
To greet you.

All past shame,
Past struggles
Once so deeply engrained,
Now long since
Dissolved, evaporated.

Annulled
By such simple surrender.

We live

We live in a world
That nurtures the illusion
All we've ever aspired to
Or indeed forsaken!
Can be swept away
When it cannot.

Like it or not,
Everything bites,
Takes its grip.

Immured
In a welter of choice
We are then.

No less,
Neither no more
Than the sum of
All we have wrought.

And this, my friend,
Is both our glory
And our shame...

See how our spirits

See how our spirits
Ebb and flow...

And with a primal energy
That fuels
These seasons of change,
The very seasons of beauty.

As ever then,
The temptation is
Not to tend your garden
Carefully enough.

Though once gold,
Always golden.

For what is life
If it is not this?

The moment
When you first catch
A glimpse
Of your better self
In the tender eyes
Of another.

And as for you,
My darling,
Cling on tight
To this very same light
And the angels
Will still come
To find you,
To save you,
To make you anew.

In turn, arriving first
As a gently
Gathering whisper.
And then,
If fully welcomed in,
Soon becoming
More like the glorious swell
Of some magnificent orchestra
Whose sole ambition
Is to stir your very soul.

And, yes indeed,
To remind you
You too have known love.

How blessed are we

To be for a while
In this,
The natural world,
Albeit
With its every whim,
Its necessary flux.

All the more so,
When no rule exists
That can even begin
To measure the scale
Of shift in spirit
Required
To make
The very best of this,
Our passage here.

I can still remember how,
When the time came,
My own mother
And indeed hers too
Took their leave
So gently, so peacefully.
A beautiful softness there.
As if to remind us
It falls to us now
To keep the faith,
To carry on giving
As joyously,
As selflessly as we can,
No matter
How many stars
Have fallen from the sky.

Warmed
By something approaching
Our capacity for wonder
In the hope they still inspire.

Oh!
To have such chances still.

For Eva...

This, a prayer of love.

Such grace, such goodness,
Such resilience.

An unquenchable spirit too.

One small hand in mine,
Bright in its wake.

I'm so glad
You're here
With me now
To share this,
The beauty of my life.

Knowing that,
With you by my side,
I will fall in love
With living again.

Each one of us,
At whatever stage
In our journey,
Possessed of a soul
That remains,
Wherever it might
Lead us,
Powerful and yet
Benevolent enough
To ensure that
With every step forward,
Even if sometimes
Tentative,
Or imperfectly made,
We will find our way
Through
To glory in the end.

Time is

Time is forever short,
When your world
Can turn in a second.

And everything,
Frail or not,
Be irreversibly
Swept away.

Yet, all the while,
Moistened
By a gaze
That's like
A soothing balm
To any such outcome,
We cannot help,
But reach
For authenticity,
For purpose,
For meaning.

Fermenting
An unending aspiration
To make the world
Anew.

In itself,
A rebellion
Against waste.

After all,
From the soiled earth
Fresh flowerings
Will come.

And in their
Glorious wake,
A re-energised belief
In redemption,
True beauty.

Life seen afresh
In iridescent
Colours of promise,
Long since hewn
From an abandoned sky.

For Maureen...

I can still recall how
It was the best feeling
In the world,
The first time
You asked me how I was,
As if it was the only thing
That mattered to you.

And at last,
Unfettered as we are,
See how far
We've come since.

Such again
Is the promise
Of tomorrow,
If we can be
Who we should be.

All we've since come
To hold dear
Adding real weight
To this, the onward journey
Of our souls.

A choice
To which we first
Exposed ourselves
In that precious moment,
Beyond any imperative
Of staying secure.

It was how
We bridged that gap.
And now, for sure my love,
We'll know of the angels
When they come for us.

It is dark now

It is dark now
And the stars
Are feasting
In the heavens.

The devil
Is in all our hearts,
My friend.

And somehow
We have to
Make our peace
With that.

The line between
The best
Of who we are,
And the darker hues
Nestled within,
As thin as gossamer,
However often it blazes…

And, at times
Like these,
It is as if God
Is in the room with us!

Our earnest faith
Still standing
As our only insurance,
Our one solid guarantor.
That, never mind
All our glittering prizes,
Neither are our moments
Of despair and desolation
Awasted too.

Our spirit

Our spirit.

Age
Does not wither it.

As if to prove,
Mortal as we are,
How splendidly
Fruitful
And piquant
We can be.

In our aspirations
At least,
Ageless as salt,
And yet
Guileless too,
Like infants.

Finely,
Though maybe
Cruelly wrought?
To dream
Only occasionally
Of the sublime.

From the darkest

From the darkest
Of shadows
Can spring forth
The brightest of light.

And how mysterious
That this can
Sometimes
Miraculously come to be.

Albeit,
More often than not,
Claimed prematurely
From ragged body,
If not full spirit.

But, in truth,
In life,
As in sex and art!

Given love
And courage too,
What thin divides
Exist
Between extremity
And any such chance
Of glorious release.

Inhibited only
By a reluctance
To reach.
A failure to dream,
To imagine.

And with such
Fine tools
At our disposal too
To inculcate the rarest,
The most radiant of pearls.

Yet how we struggle still,
As we are meant to perhaps!
To turn ourselves into Gods.

Yearning ever more
For an elevated presence
That might linger
Long after
We are done here.

And certainly,
Such are all our heroes,
No vestige
Of impermanence there.

Glistening
At the very core,
Of their unique triumph,
The essence of all
They struggled
And suffered to give.

Not one iota of doubt
What shimmers
Of divine presence
They, at least,
Leave behind them.

How chilling

How chilling
That tragedy
Can strike at any time
And seemingly
So often
With such careless
Abandon.

This we are all,
At least,
Familiar witness to.

Tempting then
To detect
In this phenomenon
The callous arrogance
Of an act of God, maybe?

Even though
The lack
Of measure,
Or indeed even
The sniff of vengeance
In its sudden unraveling,
Tells you this surely
Cannot be so.

Especially when,
Come what may,
And for a purpose
The soul
Can steadily digest,
But will never
Have full sight of,
This, our very own journey,
Simply rolls on.

Confirming,
In the absence
Of any such dogma,
We cannot help
But remain
Persistently alive.

Beacons of hope
For better days ahead.

Like some

Like some flutter
Of a fishing line,
Whose glistening hook
You've already
Been caught upon,
Don't ever look to
Undervalue suffering
When it comes to visit.

Equal as it is
To any kinder, softer,
Sweeter experience.

For, taken altogether,
This is how
We are nourished.

How we grow into
The glorious spaces
In between,
Till some vital sense
Of mystery
Is at last dissolved,
The sun glints again
Through the forest
And our hearts are captured
In a blaze of joy
And aching melancholy,
Like a memory of heaven.

From that moment on,
We become seekers.

And see how often
We lay down
To make beauty.
Then let it all go again
Longingly
Trusting that these,
Our devotions,
Will somehow always endure.

With an acknowledgement
to Peter Matthiessen

My friend

My friend,
We've all
Been here before
And know
Exactly how it is.

So often
Weighed down
By hefty,
Rough-hewn blocks
Of regret,
Marbled through
With pain and loneliness.

But don't ever
Be afraid of this,
Your shame.

Even if
No one else
Around you
Ever seems at all
Eager to claim
Their own share
Of blood
In the water!

For to acknowledge
And then faithfully
Follow instead
Its flecked
And sanguine path
Is at least to begin
To reacquaint yourself
With some form
Of open acceptance.

A healing
That may well
Start in flutters,
Artfully cajoling you
Back towards
The very core
Of your being.

A sacred place
Where,
If you have ever
Wronged your dreams,
You still have
A chance to return
To the silken thread
Of your very own dance
And be swirling in light,
Once again.

Fondly
Reliving times
When loving,
And therefore
Disposed of need,
You were the best
That you could be.

When I am

When I am
As I am,
My beliefs
Gather in strength
Like swathes
Of glorious flowers,
With delicate veins of iron.

But when I am not.
And far closer
Instead
To a tarnished apathy,
That forever smolders
Under glutinous
Layers of time,
What a poor servant
To life,
A minion of misery
I become.

My muted cries
For solace
Progressively
Compacted
Like layers of
Atrophied rock,
Hope long gone.

Better then
That my spirit
Remains fluid
And supple enough
To yearn for
Fresh experience.

This a story
I've been told to tell you.
And it's one of triumph,
With an eternal narrative
Of real worth
That is forever playing out.

After all, my friend,
Who are we anyway?
If not the extraordinary
Unearthed from the dross.

Here we are

Here we are,
At times
Almost haunted,
It seems.

Underpinned
By a faith, a feeling,
A connection.
But to what?

An inbuilt tryst,
The irreducible
Essence
Of something
So vibrant,
Yet so illusive.

Especially
When you look
To clasp on tight
And claim it
As your own.

This, the honeyed milk
That carries
The gift of a day.

A debt
We can never
Pay back,
Only acknowledge.

And, in living joyfully
And generously,
Honour as best we can.

All the while
Being defined
By who we are
And who we are not.

Part awakened...

At times
The most glorious,
Yet the most
Wayward of beings too.

Memories

Memories
Fold like strata.
Layer upon layer,
Compacted down firmly
In the very core
Of who we are.

And it's here,
In sealed pockets
Of space,
That precious energies
Pool.

Sufficiently distilled
To delve in deep
And rediscover yourself,
To even replenish time
That's gone and been lost!

Let it breathe,
Let it sing again.

Not without cost, though.

Soon to be reacquainted
With the bitter taste
Of suffering and loss,
Before wonder unfolds.

The miracle
Of how all the scars
We've ever garnered,
If allowed to
To become raw,
Relevant again,
Gradually prompt
The bold and the beautiful
Back into being.

This a lesson
The wise ones
Have always sought
To teach us.

The delight
Of such divinity within.

Believe in this place

Believe in this place,
This charmed realm of ours.

For whilst
The heavens above
Play host
To variant voices,
Whatever still tumbles on
So freely down the hill
Is here for everyone of us,
My friend.

Dazzling proof,
Whatever the vagaries,
Of the future,
Or indeed
Follies of the past!
The core abundance,
The astonishing generosity
Of life remains.

And in the shape
Of many opportunities
Still to be mined...

Miracles out there
To be found.
To feel and witness,
To claim joyously
As our own.

The most telling
Of reminders
That despite
All our struggles
And self-doubt,
The seemingly endless
Huff and puff!

Deep, deep down
In our hearts,
We are pure enough.

Much as we first
Found ourselves,
Aren't we?

Here we are then

Here we are then,
Navigating our lives
Along a winding trail,
Often beset
With such risk and remorse.

Knowing,
As we all do,
Blooms
That flower
In the harshest
Of conditions,
Are often the rarest
And most beautiful
Of all.

Now there's
A root truth for you
And forever a reason
To begin again.

To keep searching
For the goodness
In ourselves,
As well as each other.

Such thoughts
A healing balm
That will always
Stream through,
Untrammeled,
Whenever we display
The open-hearted courage
To willingly accept
Our broad wounds too.

Brimming and flush,
Like a ripe pomegranate,
Ready to shower upon us
The juiciest, the sweetest,
Most fruitful of seeds.

Succor for our spirits,
So we might rise,
Cleansed and refreshed,
To be born again.

There are fixed

There are fixed
Points of stasis here.

Lines, paths,
Boundaries,
Measures
That at least
Makes some sense
Of the physical world.

Between which
We, as open
And dynamic spirits,
Are cast
Unceremoniously
Adrift into.

Entirely
Free to move on.

To journey
Through oceans
Of doubt
And often
Daunting terrain too,
Looking to fashion
Our own way forward.

Much
As an adventurer,
Or aspiring young lover
Would.

In our hearts a yearning...

A bright stream
Bubbling up
That has still
To spring forth
And fully run
Its course.

For we have yet
To find her...

Our way.

The world

The world can be
A harsh place.

No surprise then
Tis our softness,
Our sensitivity,
The very essence
Of our anima
Which,
Often unnoticed,
Serves us so well.

So integral
To our purpose then.

And with
It's sanction
Of kindness
And restraint,
Comes the hope
Of arriving
Safely and soundly
At halcyon days.

Though,
By sometime
Sheltering so,
Just who or what
Is the custodian
Of all the glorious
Moments
That then escape us?
I often find myself
Wondering.

And will they?
Could they?
Ever possibly return
To the landscape
Of our heart
To bless us again.

Would that
We knew this,
In this life
Or indeed the next,
My friend.

For surely
Such energies
Cannot simply
Melt away
Into nothing.

Their moment
Will come again.

Perhaps,
This time round,
In the tender
And knowing hands
Of our betters.

Oh, that we might
Ever even begin
To deserve
Such certainty.

With our hearts

With our hearts open,
We can be far stronger
Than we know.

Just like that
Tarnished pane of glass
In a once faceless
And solid prison door,
Through which,
Life can now
Be viewed afresh.

Yes, we too,
Fleeting as we are,
Can still replenish
Our sunshine.
And maybe even
Hope to alight
Momentarily
Upon something
Resembling a new truth.

A step closer to Nirvana...

Till all, at last,
Is made plain.

The true kernel
Of our dilemma exposed.

And thereby beats
The fluttering pulse
Of so many
Long-cherished dreams,
Still to be realized in this,
Our very own narrow
Slither of space
Between life and death.

Where, believe me,
And far too often
Unappreciated,
All the wounds
We have hereby incurred,
On our journey to date,
Forever shape
Their blessings upon us too.

www.ingramcontent.com/pod-product-compliance
Lightning Source LLC
Chambersburg PA
CBHW032127050726
47590CB00008B/2994

* 9 7 8 0 9 9 2 7 0 9 3 3 4 *